Love in Silhouette
Poems

Love in Silhouette

Poems

T. L. Cooper

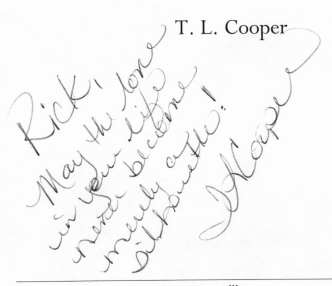

Rick,
May th love
in your life
never become
merely a
silhouette!
T Cooper

DEDICATION

I dedicate this book to all those who inspired the poems located between its covers. While our time together may not have lasted or even truly begun, the moments we shared taught me to understand, appreciate, recognize, and cherish love without expecting perfection.

ACKNOWLEDGMENTS

Poets spend many hours writing alone, but poets, like everyone, rely on other people to provide feedback and encouragement. I am fortunate to have many people who offer me unconditional support and honesty. I turned to a trusted group of friends and colleagues for feedback on myriad aspects of Love in Silhouette as I turned my vision into reality.

Much gratitude, appreciation, and love to my husband, Loay Abu-Husein, for his love, support and faith in me. His talent, knowledge, and skills helped me bring my vision for the cover into reality.

Friends, Kelly Deaton, Lori Felmey, and Bryan Rader offered invaluable feedback on both individual poems and the cover. I really appreciate their time, attention to detail, honesty, and friendship! Thanks for reminding me that great is actually better than perfect!

Authors, Stacey Rourke, Joanne Pence, Pari Noskin Taichert, LJ Sellers, John Sibley Williams and Rick Smith II earned my eternal gratitude with thoughtful, honest, thought provoking and helpful comments regarding myriad aspects of the book.

Many thanks to Trish Heath, my hair stylist, for providing her reaction to the cover and for polling the people in Destinations Hair Salon for theirs.

I'm grateful to Maureen Clifford for inviting me to read my poetry for Third Thursday Poets thus inspiring me to share my poetry with the world.

Everlasting love and gratitude to the friends and family who have been there to prop me up when love's path became treacherous.

Sincere thanks to you, my readers, for taking a chance that contained within these pages might be words to help, encourage, inspire, or at least entertain.

Love

Love
Weaves two lives into one
Binds two hearts together
Connects two souls

Love
Brings hope to life
Opens the heart to change
Comforts the soul

Love
Inspires
Rejuvenates
Invigorates

Breathed You

I breathed you in to my heart
Invited you to
Fill the empty spots
Replace the destroyed parts
Repair the damaged areas

I breathed you in to my heart
Allowed you to
Change my life
Teach me to accept love
Show me life's possibilities

I breathed you in to my heart
Trusted you to
Cherish me
Accept all of me – the loveable and the despicable
Hold my heart with tenderness

I breathed you in to my heart
Welcomed your
Comforting embrace
Insightful perspective
Loving attentiveness

I breathed you in to my heart
Where you took up residence
Gave me hope
Drove away my past
Claimed your hold

I breathed you in to my heart
Where you remain
Reminding me of happy moments

Taunting me with our mistakes
Driving me to fantasize possibilities

I breathed you in to my heart
Where you linger still
Where you refuse to leave
Where I hold you with all my strength
I breathed you in to my heart

My Heart Expanded

Today
My heart expanded
To let you in
I know not why
Only that I felt the expansion
Even as I fought it
Perhaps you need my love
Perhaps I need yours
Perhaps you desire my compassion
Perhaps I desire yours
Perhaps you want my understanding
Perhaps I want yours

Yesterday
My heart felt satiated
When you knocked on its door
I wanted desperately
To meet your requests
But I turned away
I feared
I had no more love to give
I feared
If I loved you
You would use me
I feared
If I gave you my compassion
You would hurt me
I feared
If I provided understanding
You would betray me

Today
My heart expanded

To let you in
I know not why
Only I felt compelled
To make room for you
To take a risk on you
To protect you
To feel all the joys
Of getting to know you
Of letting you know me

Yesterday
My heart said
I have enough
Why risk anything on someone new

Today
My heart said
You always have room
To give more love

Yesterday
Was just
The past interfering
With its fears

So
Today
My heart expanded
To let you in

Sequence

A smile
Talking awhile
Holding hands
Walking on the sand
Laughing aloud
Avoiding a crowd
A frown
Slowing down
Going astray
Moving away
It's over
Crying forever
Pain ends
Starting again

A Touch

Yesterday
You touched me
Today
You love me
Tomorrow
You'll need me
Someday
You'll want me
Question is
Yesterday
Did I touch you?
Today
Do I love you?
Tomorrow
Will I need you?
Someday
Will I want you?

Yesterday
I touched you
Today
I love you
Tomorrow
I'll need you
Someday
I'll want you
Question is
Yesterday
Did you touch me?
Today
Do you love me?
Tomorrow
Will you need me?

7

Someday
Will you want me?

Yesterday
We touched each other
Today
We loved one another
Tomorrow
We'll need each other
Someday
We'll want one another

Or is
A touch just a touch
With no future, past, or even present

My Heart

I gave my heart to you
With pleasure
Our love was true
You seemed like a treasure

You held my heart
With tenderness
Since it had been torn apart
By lack of kindness

My heart mended
With your love
I soon concluded
You were sent from heaven above

Then with the end
My heart was broken
Never to mend
Never again to be given.

Whole

When I open my eyes
I see your face
Your eyes say you love me
When I open my ears
I hear your voice
Your words say you'll always be here
When I open my arms
I feel your embrace
Your touch says forever true
When I open my heart
Your presence fills me
I am whole

Rain

Rain is strange
Like love.
Both are sometimes
Relaxing
Sometimes scary.
Both with storms
Lightening and
Thunder.
Exciting or
Sometimes like
A gentle shower
In the summer.

Knowing You Love Me

I see your face
We smile
I gave you space
For a while

You walk my way
I feel tears
I hope you stay
But I'm full of fear

You take my hand
I'm starting to shiver
I know you understand
All I have to deliver

As I feel your hug
I feel relief
Your hold is snug
I sigh in disbelief

As our lips touch
I'm free
I've never had so much
Knowing you love me.

My Memory

My memory
Still holds you tight
All through the night

My memory
Holds your hand
As we walk on the sand

My memory
Sees your smile
As we talk for awhile

My memory
Feels your eyes
Knowing there are no lies

My memory
Tastes your lips
As they touch my lips

My memory
Hears you talk
As we sit and rock

My reality
Is my cry
As you die...

Thoughts of You

The trees sway
My thoughts stray
I think of you
I should be blue
I smile
No clouds for awhile
The wind blows
And I know
You'll be back to me
As you realize what we can be.

Wilted

Has our love wilted
Like a dying flower
Or did you ever really care
I cared about you
And I still do
If you don't love me
I guess our love
Has wilted away
Like a dying flower.
If you don't care
If your love for me is gone
Then why should I try to
Keep our flower alive
I can't do it alone
Our flower is wilting
Slowly, slowly
Wilting away
Our flower is almost completely wilted
Almost dead now
Help me keep it alive, please.
Don't let it wilt away, please....

Forbidden

The heart feels
What it will
The mind
Can't stop it
No matter the cost
No matter the pain
No matter the price

First appeared on AssociatedContent.com

You vs. Him

I'm with you
But he owns my heart
I don't know what to do
I can't give you my heart

You can have my body
But he has my soul
I'm sorry
I have to leave you cold

I want you to be there
But he has my love
I'll never care
I have to leave you alone

It's wrong
It's right
We're only a song
In the night

Facing the end
Was not so hard
Nothing to mend
No broken hearts

Temporary

I reach for you
In the night
I feel blue
I know it's not right

You are there
To hold me
I don't care
If you set me free

My heart is cold
Unable to give
I'll grow old
Alone I'll live

You are temporary
Nothing is forever
It won't vary
We'll soon be over

No gain
Nothing lost
No pain
So little cost

Together

Others say
Forget him
I say
Forget them

They tell me
To move away
I don't agree
I want to stay

Some tell you
To forget me
But you know it's true
Your heart is not free

As we listen to our hearts
It becomes clear
We cannot stay apart
Because our love is so dear

Let's hold on to our love
Let it be real again
We don't have to give up
Because of the past pain

Your Memory

Your memory so securely
Had I put away
To come back and cruelly
Cloud my sunny days.
Time alone hasn't erased
Many of the feelings
I felt for you.

Forgetting

As she walked along
Trying to forget the love
They had shared
Loving memories
Flooded back
She fought
Back tears
And stopped
Beside his stone
She could no longer
Contain the tears.
She dropped to her knees
And placed a single red rose
On the grave.
Then she cried until
Her eyes were dry.

Complexity

Your simplicity
Couldn't conceive of
My complexity

So you picked
The parts of me
That pleased you
My smile
My eyes
My beauty
My intelligence
My generous heart
My sweetness
My willingness
My accepting nature
My lovingness
My honesty

Your simplicity
Couldn't conceive of
My complexity

So you ignored
The parts of me
You found distasteful
My bluntness bordering on cruelty
My inability to trust
My need to keep secrets
My protective wall surrounding my heart
My self-centered ambition
My biting sense of humor
My unwillingness to appear as vulnerable as I felt
My need to control

My insecurities
My damages

In the moment
Your simplicity
Crashed into
My complexity
Our true selves escaped the façade we'd built
Harsh words seared scars on our hearts
Actions betrayed secrets shared
Pain was inevitable
Our end unavoidable

My complexity
Destroyed
Your simplicity

My complexity
Created
Your complexity
To destroy
The next person's simplicity
Just as my simplicity
Had been destroyed
By another's complexity
Creating
My complexity

Your simplicity
Couldn't conceive of
My complexity

Nice Guys Don't Like Me

I wear a red dress
You have on a red tie
The color of power
We both know
I project a power I don't feel
And wonder if you're doing the same
We're both too young to know any better
I walk down the stairs to the banquet
I search the crowd for your face
You smile at me
Your eyes and smile so expressive
You're so honest about your feelings
You somehow disarm me for a moment
You like me
What's wrong with you?
Nice guys don't like me – ever
I feel so damaged, so impure, so unworthy
I strike out at
Your innocence, lack of guile, kind nature
You want to save me
But I can't be saved
I'm not worth saving
Victimization and cynicism consume
My heart, mind, and body
Doubt I can live any other way

I sit behind a desk
A romantic gesture
Two young boys march toward me single file
Each holding a rose so yellow, so pure, so perfect
You follow with a rose so red, so beautiful, so powerful
The color of power
We both know

I'm sure I ruin the moment
I'm touched beyond belief
I almost cry
I don't know how to react
To such sweetness, such romance
What's wrong with you?
Nice guys don't like me - ever
My first roses from a man
Memorialized in photos
Pressed and dried in my Bible
The red one survives
To this day
The color of power
We both know

A late night walk
A playful gesture
You jump out behind me
Frighten me
My hands close around your throat
Darkness is all I see
When it clears
There's your face
Your eyes filled with concern, not fear
Red marks on your neck
The color of power
We both know
I run away
How can I ever forgive myself?
Yet somehow you forgive me
We both manage to blame you
Unbelievably, unfairly, unreasonably
What's wrong with you?
Nice guys don't like me – ever
Driving you away proves difficult

At the time I didn't even know it was my goal

A small, pale scar on my arm
Serves as a reminder
You're ironing a shirt
I reach across in a mocking gesture
I'm determined to never iron for anybody
The iron makes slight contact
With my arm
I quickly hide the burn
Not realizing
Our relaxing yet exhilarating
Soak in a hot tub
Will exacerbate the tiny burn
A red line forms
The color of power
We both know
Your annoyance that I hid the burn
Your concern over my well being
Surprises me
It's just a little thing
I'm embarrassed by my carelessness
I'm uncomfortable that you care
What's wrong with you?
Nice guys don't like me – ever

Can't you see
I'm damaged goods
I can't be saved
I can't be loved
I can't be trusted
You could do so much better

Can't you see
I could never be

Who you think you see
What you want me to be
The woman you deserve

Yet you saved me
Without either of us knowing it
If you hadn't shown me
Something different than I knew
I wouldn't be here today
I wouldn't have learned
To accept good
To want life
What I didn't want to be

I wouldn't have realized
Vulnerability isn't weakness
Tough exteriors fail to protect
Caring doesn't have to hurt
My words and actions can inflict pain
I can be forgiven
I can be trustworthy
I can like me
I can like a nice guy

I wouldn't have discovered
While no one could save me
I could save myself
And I could accept
Assistance, comfort, and affection
Who I was didn't dictate who I became

I wouldn't have accepted
Red is just a color
To which we assign the power
Power comes from within

Power isn't everything
Nothing was wrong with you
A nice guy could like me – forever

So this morning
I cried
For the girl I was
For the nice guy I hurt
For what we thought we knew
We were too young to know any better
Then I smiled
For the woman I've become
One who could apologize
And mean it
For the man you've matured into
A man who responded to my apology with
"A life without hurt is a life not truly appreciating happiness."
Because about that we can agree, my friend

If I Had Known

I like to think
If I'd known
I'd have made
Your first time
A special event
Eased your uncertainty
Guided you on the way
Waited for just the right time
Shown you patience
Given you latitude
Celebrated the moment
Created a special evening
Made it a fantasy come true

You seemed so confident
Almost cocky
I didn't have a clue
Perhaps
I was too self-absorbed
To notice
Your nervous energy
Your momentary hesitation
The question in your eyes
Your innocence
Perhaps
I was too self-centered
To understand
The moments that followed
The attitude I'd never seen before
Your hurried excitement
What you needed from me

Your lack of trust

To tell me beforehand
Hurt but was understandable
At least I understand it now
That I learned I was your first
From another girl
After the fact
Splintered my heart
I lashed out
Instead of trying to understand
My insecurities took over
Destroyed any chance at salvaging us

Maybe you were right
Not to trust me
Maybe I would've
Spoken cruel words
Made you feel inadequate
Run away from you
Pushed you to leave me
Used your innocence against you
Hurt you worse
I like to think not
But maybe I'm trying
To rewrite me
Twenty years ago
With today's me

I like to think
If I'd known
I'd have
Appreciated the honor
Shown you understanding
Showered you with gentleness
Encouraged your talent
Given you a fair chance

Like you did so many times, so many ways, for me

The reality is
We'll never know
Because I didn't know
So the moment we created
Is the memory we possess

Your Voice

I struggle to remember
Your voice
Yet those few words
Spoken so long ago in anger
Ring through my mind with undue clarity
I wish I could forget them
They don't define who you are
Only how far I pushed you

Over time my memory has dulled
Your voice
Yet I remember
When hearing you speak
Soothed my troubled heart and soul
I long to remember how you sounded
When you spoke words
From your heart

I close my eyes and try to recreate
Your voice
Those angry words get in the way
And I struggle to release them
They were retaliation
For accusations I'd lobbed unfairly
I don't blame you for saying them
But they block all the other words

I listen to the silence hoping
Your voice
Will surface and make me smile
Like it did so many times
Before that one time
And after that one time

I wish those words you spoke
Would cease to interfere with my memories of your voice

I wonder
Would I recognize
Your voice
Should I hear it
In some random place
At some random time
Or would I go on my way
Never knowing you were nearby

I thought I heard
Your voice
Once
I turned and looked
Maybe it was even you
But I didn't have the courage to approach
I feared if it was you you'd turn your back on me
Or that you would smile that irresistible smile and embrace me

I wonder if
Your voice
Changed with age
If I heard it would I suddenly remember
Not only your voice but things better left forgotten
Or is it so altered I wouldn't know the difference
Would it still sooth me

I want to remember
Your voice
Remember more than those angry words
Remember the laughter I believe was there
Remember the care I think you tone held
Feel the openness you projected when you spoke

Hear your determination in your words
Embrace the understanding you always gave

I want to hear
Your voice
That's the heart of the matter
Maybe it's too fill in the blanks in my memory
Or to drown out those angry words once and for all
Maybe it's to convince myself we really did talk
Maybe it's to know you really are happy
Or maybe it's just plain selfishness

Echo

I hear an
Echo
No sweeter words
Have fallen upon these ears
No kinder gesture
Has been made to this soul
No gentler communiqué
Has been read by these eyes
No more memorable comment
Has come to rest in this mind
No more heart-touching exchange
Has graced this battered heart
No more uplifting sentiment
Has brought beauty to this life
Those words
Echo
Through my mind, my heart, my being
I only wish I'd heard your voice speak them
Instead of my eyes reading them
My future may have been changed by those innocent words
That continue to reverberate through my being
Such a beautiful
Echo
"I am just sad."
"Why?"
"I want you happy."

Silence Screams

Your silence screams
Echoing inside my head
Like a voice bouncing off canyon walls
My imagination reels
Wondering what I did to mute you
My thoughts dissect
Every communication for offenses
My memory replays
Every interaction for missteps

Your silence screams
Crashing though my heart
Like waves on a beach during a storm
My emotions collide
With uncertainty
My fears
Reawaken dormant insecurities
My memory
Recognizes emotions from the past

Your silence screams
Haunting my soul
Like ghosts from another lifetime
My former behavior
Returned to me
My long changed attitude
Ringing through your silence
My long forgotten fear
That vulnerability is the enemy who brings pain

Your silence screams
I cover my ears
To shut it out

But it's in my head
I cover my eyes
To block the image
But it's in my head
I clamp my mouth shut
To avoid breaking the silence that is yours to cease
But it's in my head
I try to pretend it doesn't matter
I try to actually not care
I try to wait patiently
For you to stop the screaming silence

Your silence screams
I strain to hear your voice through it
I look for hints in the nothingness
I create explanations inside my mind
I feel in spite of myself
I look for a clue the silence will end

Your silence screams
I fear I'll misunderstand the message
The silence sends
I fear your intention will be lost
In my interpretation of your silence
I search for signs in the ether
To send me in the right direction

Your silence screams
All I can do is wait
But waiting doesn't come natural to me
What comes next is up to you
So I
Nurture silent, unshed tears
In the
Bloodcurdling scream of your silence

When We Were a We

When we were a we
I loved you
The words
Never passed my lips
Remained hidden even from me
The love was no less true

When we were a we
I adored you
The words
Remained unspoken
Unrecognized by me
The adoration was no less true

When we were a we
I trusted you
The words
Unspeakable in my world
Incomprehensible to me
The trust was no less true

When we were a we
I needed you
The words
Too vulnerable for expression
Hidden deep in my heart
The need was no less true

When we were a we
I wanted you
The words
Stuck in my throat
Heart pounded to keep them concealed

The desire was no less true

When we were a we
I desired a future with you
The words
Never found form in my mind
The thought shattered every time they tried
The dream was no less real

When we were a we
Walking away was easier than expressing
The words
To make you stay
To make you want me
To make you trust me
To make you need me
To make you love me
To be vulnerable
To risk your rejection of me
The emotions were no less true

When we were a we
Losing the possibility of us splintered my heart
Risking the potential of us terrified me
So why is walking away now
When there is no possibility of us
So much harder
Than
When we were a we

Let Me Go

You don't leave my mind
Or my heart
I can't seem to find
A new start

You are a part of me
After all we've shared
How can it be
That you never cared

I've been trying for awhile
But I know
Your touch, your smile
Won't ever let me go.

Bright and New

The day dawns bright and new
What shall I do?
My heart feels old and used
My body feels sore and abused

Where do I go?
What do I know?
My heart has seeds to sow
My soul needs to grow

The day dawns bright and new
I smile thinking of you
Today is a whole new start
For my mended heart

Nothing can go wrong
Our love is too strong
Growing together
We can last forever

The day dawns bright and new...

Brand New

My heart cries
My fear dies

You move to me
How should I be?

You smile
I smile

You hold my hand
I feel a silent, sweet demand

You kiss my forehead
My cheeks turn red

Your finger slides down my face
I'm in a daze

You hug me
I feel free

Our lips touch
I've never felt so much

I long for you
As I feel brand new

The First Time

The first time
My eyes fell on you
My heart skipped a beat

The first time
You looked my way
I felt faint

The first time
Our eyes met
I felt our hearts connect

The first time
You smiled at me
My soul soared free

The first time
I heard your voice
I knew my life was about to change

The first time
You held my hand
My skin tingled with pleasure

The first time
Your lips touched mine
My heart raced

The first time
You held me in your arms
I knew I was at home
The first time
You caressed me

The sweetness overwhelmed me

The first time
We made love
Paradise took up residence in me

The first time
You said, "I love you"
My heart felt it would burst with joy

And today when…
I see you
You look at me
Our eyes meet
You smile at me
I hear you speak
You hold my hand
You kiss me
You hold me
You caress me
We make love
You say, "I love you"
I tear up because
It still feels just like…
The First Time

Two Simple Words

"Good night"
Two simple words
Said every day
By millions around the world
Two simple words
Used to end the day
Two simple words
Said by two strangers
Often almost as an afterthought
"Good night"
Two simple words
Hastily spoken by a college girl
To a man
She needed to meet
Two simple words
Replied by that handsome man
Two simple words
Connecting two hearts
Two simple words
Creating a beginning
Two simple words
Who could've known they'd mean so much
"Good night"

Two Worlds

Two worlds
Full of strife
Brought together
By two lives

Two worlds
In opposition
Of one another
Combined by affection

Two worlds
Far apart
From each other
Joined in two hearts

Two lives
Finding separation
By their worlds
Destroying their affection.

When You Smile

When you smile
My heart weeps
Your love for me is so evident in your eyes
I ache remembering
Harsh words we've exchanged
Moments of hurtful behavior
Flashes of hateful silence
I reach out for your hand
When you smile at me
My heart thumps erratically
Your acceptance of me is so evident in your eyes
I rejoice remembering
Expressions of love we've shared
Happy moments we've experienced together
Stretches of comfortable silence
When you smile
Love fills my heart
Your dedication to me shines in your eyes
For all the times we've forgiven
When it would've been easier to leave
And all the times we've held each other
Until the pain subsided
And all the times we've listened and actually heard
Just what the other needed
While the past
Holds both good and bad
And the future
Looms ahead filled with unknown moments
Today we have each other
As I'm reminded
When you smile

Broken Heart

You took a broken heart
And made it well
I knew from the start
When I fell
I gave you my best
It wasn't enough
You wanted the rest
I was too tough
You let me go
But I know
I'll always love you
Yes, I know
You'll always love me
We're apart
But never in our hearts.

I Have No Right

I have no right
I walked away
I decided on a different route
I embraced the life I desired
A life without you

I have no right
But
I want to know
Where you are
What you're doing
If life treats you well
Did you find someone to give you what I couldn't?

I have no right
But
I wonder
Do you ever think about me?
If a memory of me surfaces
Do you smile or wince
Do you hold the memory tight
Or force it away
Do you care if I found someone to give me what you couldn't?

I have no right
Yet
I smile
When memories of you surface
Because I cherish what you brought to my life
Because I hold secret little parts of what we shared
Because the bad moments of us don't seem so bad anymore
Because though it couldn't last, it was for a while
And that's enough

I have no right
However
I search for a moment
To show you I know how to be happy
To tell you how you helped me
To let you know I'm glad you were once in my life
To say I'm strong now
To explain why I had to leave

I have no right
Still
I miss our friendship
I long to make your bad moments all better
I want to share your triumphs and failures
I wish I could hug you again
I want to take back the pain I inflicted
I need you to understand why my departure was best for us both

I have no right
After
The choice I made
The way I treated you
My selfishness
My neediness
My disappearance
My lack of concern for your feelings

I have no right
But
I want to ask
Do you ever miss me?
What did you want us to be?
Why did you let me go so easily?
Why didn't you ask me to stay, just ask?

Not that it would've changed my decision — I don't think
Can you forgive me?

I have no right…

Belongs

There's a pain in my heart
 It belongs to you
You left it there
Abandoned it without a second glance
I watched but didn't try to stop you
I feel it
Teasing, taunting
Reminding
I took it on
I thought I deserved it
Maybe I did
I thought I didn't have the right to my own pain
At least where you were concerned
So I grasped
The pain you left me
Nurtured it
Caressed it
Loved it
Fed it
Pretended if I felt it
You wouldn't
You didn't
Pretended my own pain didn't exist
In the recesses of my heart
Yours was more important
Mine had no right to life
There's a pain in my heart
That belongs to us…

Void

In the void
That used to be my heart
The nothingness you left dwells
Ghosts of us haunt me
Shadows of your love sway uneasily
Memories tempt me but can't hold form
Darkness eclipses the sun of your smile
Demons of regret possess my emotions
Thieves steal our loving words
Con artists replace our truth with falsehood
When I stare into the void
I long to fill it with
Something, anything
I reach out to strangers
For the attention I want from you
I look to old friends
To distract me
I look for love, admiration, adoration
In every connection, no matter how remote
Regardless of what action I take
The void left behind by you
Remains
I don't know how to fill it
With something real
So I accept
One substitute and then another
In feeble attempts to
Fill the void
Where my heart resided
Where love encompassed and expanded
Where our future sparkled like a diamond
Where now there is only
The void

Broke My Own Heart

I broke my own heart
You offered unconditional love
I rejected it because I couldn't believe it
You wanted my all
I held my truth secret
Fearful of being vulnerable
Convinced you wouldn't love me if you knew
Then you knew and didn't run
That terrified me
I waited for you to hurt me
Instead
You only held me tighter
Coaxed laughter from me
Massaged away my tension
Wiped away my tears
Listened to my ranting
Traced my reluctant smile with your finger
Until the reluctance dissipated
In the end
I broke your heart
I broke my own heart
Because I couldn't accept that I deserved love
Because I couldn't believe anyone could love me
Because I thought it best for you if I left
I broke my own heart
I chose the option that proclaimed love didn't exist
I chose rejection of my truth
I chose the place where I could hide
From love
From truth
From you
From me
From the world

I broke my own heart

If We Loved Once

If you loved me once
Could you love me again
Can you remember
Why you loved me
Can you forget
What drove us apart
Can you open yourself to me
Can you forgive my mistakes
Am I worth the risk

If I loved you once
Can I love you again
I remember
Every reason I loved you
I'll never forget
How I drove you away
This time I'll be vulnerable to you
I'll forgive your mistakes
You are worth the risk

If you loved me once
Could you love me again
Is the pain of our past
Too much to overcome
Is the disappointment
Too much to resolve
Is my lack of trust
Too difficult to pardon
If I loved you once
Can I love you again
I vow to release
The pain of our past
I vow to resolve

The disappointment we created
This time I promise to trust you
If you'll give me the chance

If you loved me once
Could you love me again
Perhaps you only loved an image
Of someone I can never be
Perhaps you only wanted
The easy to love parts of me
Perhaps when that image shattered
You realized you never loved me

If I loved you once
Can I love you again
Perhaps I saw something in you
That never really existed
Perhaps I could only
Handle the easy to love parts of you
Perhaps when my image of you shattered
I decided I never really loved you

If you loved me once
Could you love me again
It's the question I have to ask
It's the answer I most fear
It's the question I can't ask
It's the answer I'll never have
Unless you answer the unspoken

If I loved you once
Can I love you again
It's the question I refuse to ask
It's the answer that terrifies me
It's the question that haunts me

It's the answer that incessantly whispers to me
No matter how much I shush it

If we loved each other once
Can we love each other again
Perhaps I was delusional
To think you ever loved me
Perhaps I was delusional
To think what I felt for you was love
Perhaps I saw what I wanted to see
When I looked in your eyes
Perhaps I created a memory
Of something that never existed

If we loved each other once
Can we love each other again
Fear stands in the way
Of being vulnerable enough to find out
Past pain creates apprehension
That splinters our hearts but keeps us silent
We flirted with the question
We ignored the answer

If we loved each other once
Can we love each other again
We'll never know
Because we fell silent to avoid the question
Because we walked away from the answer
When the question refused to be silenced
Inside our hearts

If you loved me once
Could you love me again
If I loved you once

Can I love you again

But what if
It was never love
It was only an illusion
It was only a fantasy
It was pretense
What if it
Fooled us both
I can't believe that
It felt too good
It felt too special
It felt too perfect
It felt too right
It felt too real

So I'll love you again
If I ever stopped

However you don't have to love me again
But could you?

At Least That's What I Tell Myself

A moment shared
With you
Is better than never knowing you
At least that's what I tell myself

A day spent laughing
With you
Is worth the tears I'm left with
At least that's what I tell myself

To know your touch
Once
Is a memory worth creating
At least that's what I tell myself

To experience your brilliant smile
Once
Is a light to hold in dark moments
At least that's what I tell myself

To spend a night in your embrace
Once
Lingers happily on my aura forever
At least that's what I tell myself

To feel the pressure of your lips on mine
A single time
Is enough to cherish for a lifetime
At least that's what I tell myself
To hear you speak my name with love
A single time
Is a song forever in my heart
At least that's what I tell myself

A moment shared
With you
Is better than never knowing you
At least that's what I tell myself

The moment
We shared
Ended
As perfect moments do

At least that's what I tell myself

Something That Isn't

We try to deny
We try to pretend
We tell ourselves it's nothing
This thing between us
Others see it
Point it out
Shake their heads
Warn us of the dangers
We accuse them of
Seeing
Something that isn't
We deny the connection we feel
We pretend our ease with one another is nothing
Yet
Every time we talk
Every time we share
Every time we connect
We have to remind ourselves
That this thing between us
That others point out is
Something that isn't
We point out
To them
To ourselves
To each other
The distance between us
The differences that define us
The reasons what was between us no longer is
Why we can't be the
Something that isn't
That others continue to shine light on
Yet in weak moments
Our hearts feel

Our minds wonder
Our bodies remember
A time when
Something that isn't
Existed
And maybe someday
We'll ask
If
When people see
Something that isn't
They're simply seeing
Something we deny
Something that terrifies us
Something that we've run from forever
Maybe then we'll see
That
Something that isn't
Is actually
Something that is

Cost You Me

If you could unsay
The words you said
If you could unwrite
The words you wrote
If you could unthink
The thoughts you thought
If you could unfeel
The emotions you felt
If you could unask
The request you made
If you could undo
The actions you took
If you could erase
The words, thoughts, emotions, request, actions that
Cost you me
Would you?
Would I even want you to?
Perhaps you said
Words that needed said
Perhaps you wrote
Words that needed written
Perhaps you thought
Thoughts that needed thought
Perhaps your request
Needed asked
Perhaps the actions you took
Needed taken
Even though the words, thoughts, emotions, request, actions
Cost you me
Perhaps losing me
Needed to happen
But still
There is a moment

Now and then
When I wonder if
You ever wonder if
The words, thoughts, emotions, request, actions that
Cost you me
Were worth the cost

Cost Me You

If I could unsay
The words I said
If I could unwrite
The words I wrote
If I could unthink
The thoughts I thought
If I could unfeel
The emotions I felt
If I could unask
The request I made
If I could undo
The actions I took
If I could erase
The words, thoughts, emotions, request, actions that
Cost me you
I would
Wouldn't I?
Maybe not
Maybe the words
Needed spoken
Maybe the words
Needed written
Maybe the thoughts
Needed thought
Maybe the emotions
Needed felt
Maybe the actions
Needed taken
Even though the words, thoughts, emotions, request, actions
Cost me you
Maybe losing you
Needed to happen
But still

There is a moment
Now and then
When I wonder if
The words, thoughts, emotions, request, actions that
Cost me you
Were worth the cost

Speak

You speak
I speak
Words carefully weighed
Words measured twice
Words deliberately melded
Expressions of truth tempered
Disagreements diluted
Agreements celebrated
Common interests exalted
Differences ignored

You speak
I speak
Words find an edge
Words strike at vulnerabilities
Words tossed out with careless abandon
Expressions of truth become brutal
Disagreements intensified
Agreements dismissed
Common interests ignored
Differences exaggerated

You speak
I speak
Words erupt with venom
Words hit their target
Words drive a wedge
Expressions of regret unspoken
Disagreements linger between
Agreements forgotten
Common interests lost
Differences focused on

You speak
I speak
Words laced with sorrow
Words search for what was
Words attempt to reunite
Expressions of remorse gently proffered
Disagreements seek compromise
Agreements sought
Common interests revisited
Differences discussed

You speak
I speak
Words know how to hurt or heal at will
Words wielded for good or bad
Words used with wisdom of one another
Expressions of love and hate
Disagreements accepted
Agreements commonplace
Common interests enjoyed
Differences rejoiced

You speak
I speak
Words filled with possibility
Words filled with knowledge
Words filled with discovery
Expressions of self
Disagreements overlooked
Agreements taken for granted
Common interests demoted
Differences ignored

You speak
I speak

Words fill the space between
Words share our beings
Words create the us we are
Expressions of unity
Disagreements bring new understanding
Agreements exulted once again
Common interests enjoyed
Differences provide insight

You speak...
I speak...

Unspoken

Words need spoken
They remain suppressed
They haunt the happy moments
They stifle the laughter
They interfere with intimacy
They intensify the bad moments
They remain unspoken
They layer on top of one another
Building a monument to the
Unspoken
Without speaking the words
Silence proclaims the distance
Bitten lips hold the fight at bay
Clenched jaws keep the truth in a vise
But at all costs
The words that need shared
The words that need heard
The words that need spoken
Remain
Unspoken

Between Us

The truth sits
Between us
Like a growing steel barrier
We avoid facing it
Go about daily life
Pretending things are different
Wishing yesterday could return
Hoping something will change
Without us torching the steel barrier
We ignore the barrier as it grows
Between us
Layer upon layer
We turn attention to the mundane
Clean out the closets
Shed excessive junk
Abandon unneeded weight
Change our residence
Redecorate the house
Occupy our days
Focus on career goals
Make small talk
Solve the world's problems
Straining to look over the top of the steel barrier
Ever-growing
Between us
Lose ourselves in entertainment
Retire to different rooms
Engage in separate activities
All in the name of exploring individuality
Ignoring the thickening steel barrier
All to avoid
The truth sitting
Between us

Cloud Cover

Dark clouds hover overhead
Infecting my thoughts of you
Shading the sunshine that is you
Threatening a downpour of destruction
I search for a break in the hovering clouds
The brightness of your smile
Would erase the cloud cover
If only I could find it

Distance

Wish it was not true
But I miss you far too much
Even though I shouldn't

Distance Two

You are there always
I am far away from you
That's how it must be

Distance Three

If you come near me
We will soon find connection
Then deconstruction

Bleeds

Melancholy bleeds from my pen
Releasing grief's grip from my heart
Disappointment reddens the ink
Obscuring the bad and the good I saw in you
Pain bleeds into my words
Freeing me from your abandonment
Anger bleeds into the empty spaces
Left by unspoken words concealing the truth
Sadness bleeds on the paper
Ripping apart the fragments we left behind
Denial bleeds into the unwritten
Allowing me to believe you still love me
Desire bleeds into the unspoken
Creating the fantasy of your embrace
Need bleeds into my dreams
Urging me to beg for the impossible
Acceptance bleeds into every expression
Providing the illusion of freedom from you
Melancholy bleeds from my pen
Releasing grief's grip from my heart

Yesterday

If this me today
Met the you of yesterday
Would we still find love

Thoughts of You

Thoughts of you
Are here to stay
Thoughts of you
Won't go away

Thoughts of you
Are in my heart
Thought of you
Make my tears start

Thoughts of you
Invade my life
Thoughts of you
Should bring me strife

Thoughts of you
Make me smile
Thoughts of you
Seem worth my while

Thoughts of you
Still make my heart sing
Thoughts of you
Still make bells ring

Thoughts of you....

Love

Love
Comes to me at dawn
Reminds me at noon
Comforts me in the evening
Fills me at midnight

Your Touch

Your touch
Thrills me
Chills me
Scares me
Excites me
Steals my control
Provides my freedom

Fingers

Your long, sexy, strong fingers
I smile as I stare at them
I can't help it
You're unaware
Your task innocent, menial even
I can't stop myself
My imagination uses
Your fingers
To stroke my hair
To trail along the curve of my jaw
To gently brush my pouting, slightly parted lips
       Which respond with a kiss almost too light for detection
Your finger
Slips toward my neck as I lift my head
Slides toward my collar bone
Hesitating slightly halfway down as I swallow
I close my eyes
Your finger
Slithers between my breasts
Wanders first to my right nipple
Then my left
Teasing until each responds with tautness
Your finger
Gently explores the curve beneath each breast
Lingering at the point between them
I smile at the touch, so light yet with such urgent appreciation
Your finger
Slows and lifts to a featherlike touch
Skimming my stomach
Passes my navel
My breath quickens
I shift slightly to hint at access
Your finger

Reaches that most desirable destination
The promise of paradise
I recognize the prized touch that melts inhibitions
I recognize the urgency that gives you complete control
I recognize the surrender my body gives to pleasure
To
Your fingers
But
I open my eyes
And see
Your fingers
Still Toiling at your innocent, menial task
You're still unaware
While my imagination took
Your fingers
On a journey
Of discovery
Of desire
Of pleasure
I sigh
Staring once again at
Your long, sexy, strong fingers

Being You

The day I met you
I had no idea
Just how much you'd change my life
You showed me joy
You taught me love
You brought me peace
You gave me life
You accepted me
Just as I was
No one had ever done that before
You showed me
That I mattered
And
Amazingly
You did all that
Just by
Being You

Marriage

Two people coming together
Pledging to build a future together
Facing the world together
Promising to lift each other up
Providing a soft landing for each other
Committing to each other's dreams
Encouraging each other when disappointments encroach
Celebrating achievements together
Crying on each other's shoulders
Laughing together
Holding each other without a reason
Kissing good morning
Hugging good night
Snuggling
Loving in good times

                            And bad

Six Months

Six months
Being your wife
Seems perfect in my life

Six months
It is so rare
To have a husband beyond compare
Six months
It is no longer new
To forever give my heart to you

Six months
My love only grows stronger
As our time together grows longer

Six months
A short time together
Compared to our future forever

To My Love

The day's end fast approaching
Though not fast enough
Can't wait to see your smiling face
Another chance to see the twinkle in your eyes
To feel your loving caress
Such warm arms to come home to
To hear your laughter
To share your joy
To comfort your pain or disappointments
To feel your kiss say it all
Thoughts of you lift my spirits in low moments
Thoughts of you bring a smile to my face
A bounce to my step
A love that never tires
An affection that never dies
The day's end is only the beginning
Over and over again

Every Day

Every day
I'm most grateful
You wake up next to me
You hold me tight
You kiss me
You love me

Every day
I'm most grateful
You were born
You came into my life
You married me
You're a part of my life today

Every day
I'm most grateful
For the
Life, love, and joy
We share

All I Need

I don't need
Midnight walks on the beach
Diamonds adorning my fingers
Crystal vases filled with roses

I don't need
Trips around the world
Fancy cars to drive
Expensive clothes to wear

All I need is
To wake beside you each morning
To feel your arms around me
To see your smile each day

All I need is
To taste your lips on mine
To feel your caress linger
To hear your laughter

All I need is
You

The Man You Are

The man you are
Brings out the best in me
Makes me strive to be a better wife
Gives me hope for the future

The friend you are
Listens when I need to be heard
Advises when I need direction
Encourages me to take a chance

The lover you are
Fills me with pleasure
Exceeds my every fantasy
Keeps me running back for more

The husband you are
Holds me when I'm weak
Loves me when I screw up
Celebrates my successes

The husband you are
The lover you are
The friend you are
The man you are
Just keeps getting better and better
Year after year

Your Presence

Your presence
In my life
Has brought me
More joy
More pleasure
More comfort
More excitement
More love
Than I could ever describe
With mere words
Than I could ever express
With a present
That I could ever
Thank you enough for
You'll never know
Just how much
My appreciation for you
Grows with each year

Marriage Routine

Morning
Waking in your arms
Surrounded by your love
Enveloped in your passion
Hugs & kisses making promises for later

Afternoon
Remembering your morning affection
Longing to hold you
Hearing your voice on the phone
Saying "I Love You"

Evening
Your kiss on my lips
Your hug embracing me
Your eyes glowing with love
Showing you've missed me

Night
A glance across the room
A sudden touch
Discussing the day
Strengthening our bond

Bedtime
Snuggling against your body
Your arms surrounding me
One last kiss of the day
You whisper "I Love You"

Weekends
Long mornings in bed
Talking and cuddling
Afternoons playing
Evenings relaxing

Our life
Together we face
Any obstacle
Each disappointment
Every struggle

Together we celebrate
Each success
Every victory
The love we share

I am so glad
We chose to walk
This path of marriage together

Thirty Seconds, Three Weeks

Squeezing three weeks
Of love
Into a thirty second hug
A kiss so intense my lips feel bruised
Breathing in your scent
Relishing your arms tightly surrounding me
Absorbing the heat of our bodies smashed together
Your whisper "I love you" tickles my ear
Watching you walk away
Taking my heart with you
Leaving me adrift
Longing for thirty more seconds
Appreciation for you causes
A teardrop to form
A knot in my throat
Guilt sets in
As I remember friends who are alone
Friends who'll never have
Even one more second
With their most cherished
I can't even imagine…
Anger sets in
As I think of
People who throw away love
As casually as a sock with a hole
I can't even imagine…
Life without you can't
Invade my imagination
Penetrate my reality
So I'll hold
Those thirty seconds close
I'll cherish the touch, the words, the love
Expressed in those thirty seconds

For the next three weeks
Until your arms
Embrace me once again
Your whisper tickles my ear
Your lips bruise mine
Your scent fills me with security
Your love is beside me
My heart settles back into place
Instead of reaching across continents
Thirty seconds will survive three weeks

As If

I asked
For your understanding
You reacted
As if
I asked you
To move a mountain with your bare hands

I asked
For you to listen
You reacted
As if
I asked you
To jump over the Grand Canyon

I asked
For you to see me
You reacted
As if
I asked you
To trek through a blizzard barefoot

I asked
For your devotion
You reacted
As if
I asked you
To drink the entire ocean in a single gulp

I asked
For your advice
You reacted
As if
I asked you

To fly through the air without wings

I asked
For your friendship
You reacted
As if
I asked you
To stop a tsunami with your body

I asked
For you to embrace me
You reacted
As if
I asked you
To traverse the desert without water

I asked
For your support
You reacted
As if
I asked you
To swim around the world naked

I asked
For a moment of your life
You reacted
As if
I asked you
To stop the Earth's rotation

I asked
For you to value me
You reacted
As if
I asked you

To redirect a hurricane from the shore

I asked
For you to walk beside me
You reacted
As if
I asked you
To halt the Earth's revolution around the sun

I asked
For you to release me
You reacted
As if
I asked you
To give me heaven

I asked
For your forgiveness
You reacted
As if
I asked you
To move the moon

I asked
For your love
You reacted
As if
I asked you
To walk through hell

I asked
You reacted
As if
So now
If you wonder

Why I'm gone
Ask yourself
If you triggered my reaction
When you reacted
As if...

Break My Heart

You break my heart
I run and hide
I escape into my fantasies
I go quiet
I try to make it make sense

You break my heart
I make excuses
I twist your words to make you right
I go quiet
I convince myself you didn't mean it

You break my heart
I swallow my pride
I accept that you meant it
I go quiet
I pretend it doesn't hurt

You break my heart
I decide I must like the pain
I know it'll happen again
I go quiet
I promise myself next time I'll be prepared

You break my heart
I swear it's the last time
I vow I'll never let you again
I go quiet
I come back for more

Redefining Common Ground

My heart longs
My memory searches
My body aches
My soul stalls
My mind seeks
Redefining common ground

Life moves along
Bringing me forward
Pushing me back
Reminding me of times together
Good and bad
Laughter and tears
Joy and heartache
Redefining common ground

Recognizing
All we've worked through
All we've changed
The moments we've experienced
The moments we've lost
The pain we've inflicted
The sacrifices
The dreams
The successes
The failures
Redefining common ground

Acknowledging
The life we've created
The differences
The commonalities
All we've learned

All we've suppressed
All we wanted
Expectations met
Expectations ignored
Experiences we can't change
Redefining common ground

Discovering
Sometimes
We still don't really know one another
A pleasant surprise
A heartbreaking truth
A joyful moment
A tear-jerking reality
An unearthed dream
A sudden revelation of inner desires
Redefining common ground

Travelling
This journey we began
This path we wander
The wrong turns
The right choices
The never ending struggle
To embrace
The reality of who we are
Together
Individually
The growth we experience
Together
Individually
The changing dreams
Shared
Individual
The altering goals

Shared
Individual
Redefining common ground

Experiencing
Moments of clarity
Minutes of uncertainty
Hours of fighting
Days of loving
Years of compromise
Remembering yesterday
Appreciating today
Planning for tomorrow
Redefining common ground

Coming together
Drifting apart
Holding on when the ground shook beneath us
Trembling when our foundation cracked
Sacrificing for happiness
Compromising to find peace
Holding fast to what works
Letting go of what fails
Finding our way together
Redefining common ground

First appeared on AssociatedContent.com

Valentine's Day

On Valentine's Day
Thoughts turn to
Love and romance
Artificial and forced
Though it may be

Expectations of
Fancy, overly expensive candlelight dinners
Chocolates and roses
Sexy lingerie and jewelry
Proposals and expressions of love
Expectations that
Lead to disappointment and hurt feelings

When people
Love fully everyday
Spend time together "just because"
Open hearts more freely
Appreciate one another consistently
Share their lives more easily
Communicate openly

They discover
Love that is true and strong
Lives in hearts and lives
Every day of the year
Expectations for that one day diminish
Making life and love fuller and richer
Everyday

First appeared on AssociatedContent.com

Love Doesn't Exist

Love doesn't exist
These words
Spoken so casually
By you
Given no more importance
Than ordering a latte
Exploded in my heart
Smothered my breath
Reverberated in my thoughts
Smashed my soul
Shattered my world
Changed my image of you
Why, I'm not sure
You'd expressed the sentiment before
Though not in those words
This time they changed everything
I finally believed you

Love doesn't exist
These words
Created
Questions I struggle to voice
If
Love doesn't exist
How can you claim
You love me
You cannot possess
What doesn't exist
You cannot give
What doesn't exist
If
Love doesn't exist
Why do you stay

How can you connect
To me, to anyone
How can you exist
If love doesn't live in your heart
If
Love doesn't exist
What motivates you
How can you awake
Each morning
How can you move forward
If
Love doesn't exist
How can anything matter
What's the point in living
Why bother putting in the effort

For me
Who believes
Love is the foundation
Of everything good and beautiful and strong
Love is where we begin
Love brings us together
Love heals broken hearts
Love mends injured souls
Love stitches lives together
Love roots us to our past
Love gives us motivation for the future
Love connects people to one another
Love elevates us to heights unknowable
Your words so casually uttered
Love doesn't exist
Feels like saying
I don't exist
-        At least to you

Love doesn't exist
I still hear those words
My mind can't quite comprehend
My heart can't quite accept
My soul can't quite believe
Yet
I hurt not only for me
But for you
To not know love
To not feel love
To not understand love's power
To need scientific proof of love's existence
To be unable to live in love
To exist without love isn't even living

And yet
When you uttered
Love doesn't exist
I finally realized
I
Can't make you feel love
Can't make you understand love
Can't change who you are
Can't change who I am
Can't love you enough
For the both of us
Can't show you enough love
To prove its existence
So
If
Love doesn't exist for you
Where does that leave us?

Look At Me

Look at me
Like you once did
Your eyes burning with passion's fire
At the sight of me
Your eyes glowing
With the desire to know me
Your eyes slowly devouring
Not only my body but my soul
Your eyes screaming
The passion you feel for me
Your gaze melting
The ice surrounding my damaged heart
Your gaze searing you
Into my heart forever
Your eyes filled with the answers
To the questions that make me sink into your embrace
Your eyes filled with acceptance
For all of me – the nice, the naughty, the average
Your eyes filled with love
At the thought of me
Look at me
Like you once did…

Love in Silhouette

A heart once rotund with joy
A body once vibrating with passion
A life once alive with hope
A relationship once perfection
Intimacy disguises flaws
Change is compromise
Dulled rationality
Brightened colors
Euphoria clouds judgment
Life travels its course
Euphoria dissipates
Colors fade
Rationality exposes the truth
Change blinds one to one's self
Perfection becomes imperfect
Flaws destroy intimacy
Hope evaporates as illusions burn to ashes
Routine drowns joy
The heart flattens as thin as tissue paper
Leaving
Love in Silhouette

ABOUT THE AUTHOR

T. L. Cooper grew up on a farm in Tollesboro, Kentucky. She earned her Bachelor of Science degree from Eastern Kentucky University in Richmond, Kentucky. Her poems, short stories, articles, and essays have appeared online, in books, and in magazines. She published a novel, *All She Ever Wanted*. When not writing, she enjoys yoga, golf, and traveling. Currently, she lives in Albany, Oregon. To learn more, visit www.tlcooper.com.